My Science Library

Run, Swim, Fly

by Julie K. Lundgren

Science Content Editor:
Kristi Lew

Rourke Publishing

www.rourkepublishing.com

Science content editor: Kristi Lew

A former high school teacher with a background in biochemistry and more than 10 years of experience in cytogenetic laboratories, Kristi Lew specializes in taking complex scientific information and making it fun and interesting for scientists and non-scientists alike. She is the author of more than 20 science books for children and teachers.

www.rourkepublishing.com

Photo credits:
Cover © Mark Beckwith, Andrei Nekrassov, Hugh Lansdown; Cover logo frog © Eric Pohl, test tube © Sergey Lazarev; Page 3 © Monkey Business Images; Page 5 © mlorenz; Page 7 © Kirsanov; Page 9 © Mark Beckwith; Page 11 © kostudio; Page 13 © Jeff Banke; Page 15 © mlorenz; Page 17 © Rich Carey; Page 19 © Andrei Nekrassov; Page 20 © SINITAR; Page 22 © Mark Beckwith, SINITAR, mlorenz; Page 23 © Kirsanov, John Carnemolla, Andrei Nekrassov

Editor: Kelli Hicks

Cover and page design by Nicola Stratford, bdpublishing.com

Library of Congress Cataloging-in-Publication Data

Lundgren, Julie K.
Run, swim, fly / Julie K. Lundgren.
p. cm. -- (My science library)
Includes bibliographical references and index.
ISBN 978-1-61741-720-7 (Hard cover) (alk. paper)
ISBN 978-1-61741-922-5 (Soft cover)
1. Animal locomotion--Juvenile literature. I. Title.
QP301.L86 2012
573.79--dc22

2011003762

Rourke Publishing
Printed in the United States of America,
North Mankato, Minnesota
060711
060711CL

www.rourkepublishing.com - rourke@rourkepublishing.com
Post Office Box 643328 Vero Beach, Florida 32964

Rourke Publishing

Children hop, run, and crawl.
How do animals move?

Some animals **fly.**
Birds fly.

Bats fly.
They fly at **night.**

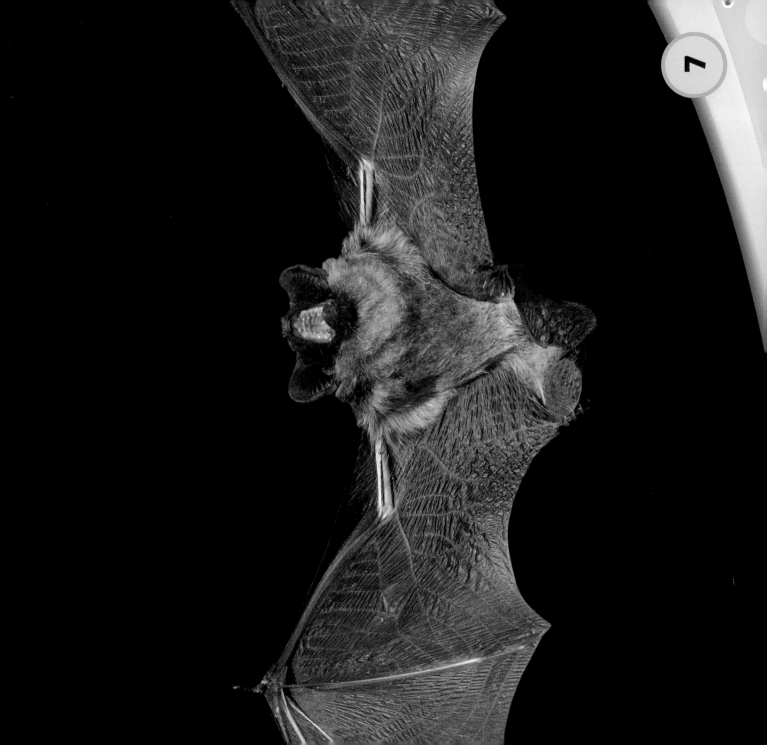

Some animals run.

Cheetahs run.

Dogs run, too.

Some animals hop.
Rabbits hop.

Kangaroos hop.

Some animals swim.
Fish swim.

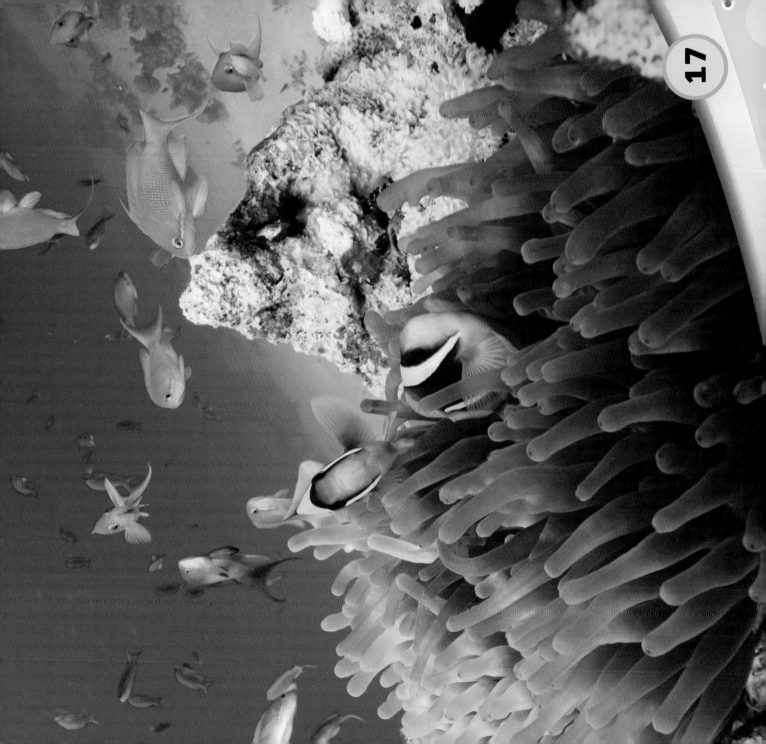

Penguins swim, too.

Who **climbs**? Who swings?
Animals move in many ways.

SHOW what you know

1. Can you name some ways animals move?

2. Do all birds fly?

3. How many ways can you move?

cheetahs (CHEE-tahz):
These large, spotted cats live in parts of Africa and Asia. They are the fastest land animals.

climbs (KLIMZ):
To climb, an animal moves up things by gripping and pulling with front legs and pushing with back legs.

fly (FLY):
Animals use their wings to flap and soar through the air.

kangaroos (kang-guh-ROOZ): These large animals live in Australia and hop easily using their strong back legs.

night (NITE): This is the dark time between sunset and sunrise.

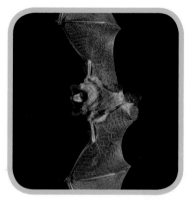

penguins (PEN-gwihnz): These flightless birds live near cold oceans and swim to catch food.

Index

fish 16
fly 4, 6
hop 3, 12, 14

penguins 18
run 3, 8, 10
swim 16, 18

Websites

www.animalfactguide.com
www.buildyourwildself.com
www.inaturalist.org

About the Author

Julie K. Lundgren grew up near Lake Superior where she liked to muck about in the woods, pick berries, and expand her rock collection. Her interests led her to a degree in biology. She lives in Minnesota with her family.